Ellen's Forgotten Mercia

To Joyce with thanks
for much help and support

Previous Publications

1993 - The Collegiate Church of St Peter Wolverhampton Guide Book
- contribution to text.
Published by R J L Smith and Associates

1995 - Under the Wing of St Peter
Published by St Peter's Church Wolverhampton

1995 - Lady Wulfrun's Hampton
Published by St Peter's Church Wolverhampton

1997 - The Fowler Legacy
Published by Brewin Books

1998 - St Peter's House
Published by St Peter's Church Wolverhampton

Ellen's Forgotten Mercia

Ellen Thorneycroft Fowler's Mershire,
including Wolverhampton, Tettenhall, Sedgley
Bridgnorth, and other local scenes in her novels

Anthony Perry

Brewin Books

Ellen's Forgotten Mercia

First Published by Brewin Books Ltd.
Studley, Warwickshire
in January 1999

ISBN 1 85858 132 X
British Library Cataloguing in Publication Data
A Catalogue record for this book is available from
The British Library

Typeset in Caxton Book
Made and printed in Great Britain
by Heron Press, Kings Norton, Birmingham

Contents

Foreword

Industrialisation transformed nineteenth century Britain. It thrust out a society that was dominated by agriculture and social hierarchy and it swept in a nation that was urban, industrial and class-based. Such a revolutionary change drew the attention of commentators from across the globe. In particular, they were attracted to the cotton district of the north west and its capital, Manchester. This great city seemed to epitomise the startling new way of things. Like Friedrich Engels, the thinker and writer who influenced Karl Marx, observers were struck by a place in which employers and workers were separated by income, politics, residence, language, attitudes, hopes and aspirations.

Foreigners were not alone in their fascination for the steam-driven textile mills of Lancashire and Cheshire. So too were English writers like Elizabeth Gaskell and Charles Dickens. With novels such as 'Hard Times' and 'North and South' they publicised the split in the nation between the manufacturing north and the more traditional south. Yet as the industrialised regions became more familiar, the interest of observers waned and they shifted their attention to the world's greatest city, London. The nation's capital appeared to encapsulate the ills which bedevilled Britain. Despite its huge wealth, the land was stalked by poverty and hunger. Nowhere was this paradox more obvious than at the heart of the empire, where only a small space cut off the rich of the west end from the poor of the east end. It was this stark division which led to social accounts by the score and to novels by George Gissing, Margaret Law and others.

Of course, there were writers who concentrated their attention on other places. Thomas Hardy, for example, detailed the dying days of the English peasantry, whilst Arnold Bennett told of life in the towns of the Potteries. Still, the main places of interest were obvious, leading to an incomplete picture of Britain. There were massive gaps in the landscape of novelists, nowhere more so than in relation to the Black Country. A region that was forged by coal, steam and iron, it received scant notice in any form of writing. An exception is the wonderfully evocative 'Walks in the Black Country', written by Elihu Burritt - the American Consul in Birmingham - as a description of the West Midlands he knew so well. For all its power, Burritt's work did not gain longstanding national recognition. The same fate befell Ellen Thorneycroft Fowler, a novelist marked out not only by her gender but also by her subject area - the western reaches of the Black Country.

Today, her name is not immediately recognisable and that is why this work by Anthony Perry is so important. He has ensured that this woman who wrote about industrial Staffordshire one hundred years ago should not sink beneath the waves of history. His researches have emphasised how deeply Ellen Thorneycroft Fowler knew places like Wolverhampton, Tettenhall and Sedgley. As a result he has made plain the historical value of her writings. This book is an important one. It should be read, not only for our understanding of Wolverhampton, Tettenhall and Sedgley but also for our understanding of the West Midlands as a whole in the nineteenth century.

DR CARL CHINN

Ellen Thorneycroft Fowler

Ellen Thorneycroft Fowler was born in 1860, at the house which is now 7 Summerfield Road, West Park, Wolverhampton. Summerfield in 1860 was just a track, with a few villas built fronting on to it, leading from Chapel Ash to the old Race Course at Broadmeadows, where the park was to be laid out some 20 years later.

Ellen's parents were Henry Hartley Fowler and Ellen Thorneycroft, who were married at the nearby Church of St Mark's, Chapel Ash, in 1857. Henry Fowler, the son of a Methodist minister, became a prominent local solicitor. He was elected a Member of Wolverhampton Council, then made Mayor by his fellow Councillors. In later years he entered Parliament to represent the town. He rose to the status of Cabinet Minister before being knighted, and was raised to the peerage as First Lord Wolverhampton. Ellen Thorneycroft was a daughter of George Thorneycroft, wealthy ironmaster and first Mayor of Wolverhampton after it was incorporated. The Thorneycrofts' house, now extended and converted to offices, can be seen as Salisbury House/Granville House, Tettenhall Road. The young Ellen was educated mainly at home, although she did go to a private school for a short time when she was in her teens. In 1867 the family moved to Woodthorne, Wergs Road, Tettenhall, a house built by Henry Fowler for himself and his family. This was demolished 20 years ago by the Ministry of Agriculture, Fisheries and Food to make way for offices. Ellen began to write at an early age, and appeared in print in her 20's, with stories and poems in magazines and periodicals. Her first books came out in the 1890's, and her first novel in 1898, "Concerning Isabel Carnaby", quickly became a best seller.

7 Summerfield Road, Wolverhampton (Photograph Joyce Perry)

Ellen Thorneycroft Fowler
(Photograph courtesy Wolverhampton Archives and Local Studies)

She built on this success with more novels appearing regularly, and this continued after she married Alfred Felkin, Schoolmaster and Schools Inspector, in 1903. They began their married life at Eltham, Kent, then in 1916 they moved to Bournemouth, where her published works became less frequent and where she died in 1929. She is buried just over the Poole boundary in the churchyard of All Saints, Branksome Park. Ellen had a brother, Henry Ernest, and a sister, Edith Henrietta. Edith also wrote novels, although she was not so prolific as Ellen, and had published a biography of their father in 1912, the year after his death.

For a more detailed account of the Fowler family, their relationship with Wolverhampton, and the writings of the two sisters, read "The Fowler Legacy" by Anthony Perry, published by Brewin Books in 1997.

Mershire

"I prefer to deal with real places, though I don't always do so. You are so apt to mislay your rivers or to lose a church if you are dealing with a place that exists solely in your own imagination."

So said Ellen Thorneycroft Fowler in an interview after the publication of her third successful novel. Certainly readers who know Wolverhampton and the surrounding districts can find real places used as settings for some of the scenes in her books. Some names of places and buildings are completely changed, others are only slightly altered and still recognisable.

Mershire is Ellen's Staffordshire, but her use of local settings extends beyond the county boundary. This book uses archive and modern photographs to illustrate Ellen's writings and hopefully encourages an interest in a long forgotten local authoress.

Whilst her books went out of fashion and were never reprinted after her death, it is still possible to find copies of her more successful early novels in second-hand and antiquarian bookshops.

Wolverhampton

(a) Queen Square

"In the very middle of the Midlands there is a manufacturing town situated on the crest of a hill and crowned by a beautiful old church. In the churchyard stands a strange pillar, the origin whereof is lost in antiquity - it may be the shaft of an early Christian cross, or it may be the remains of a Druidical temple; and just outside the lych-gates is the King's Square, with its wide pavements and quaint old shops - shops which have remained in the same families of worthy burgesses from generation to generation. The streets slope away from the square, and gradually die away into the country, which is bounded by a distant rim of low blue hills. Such is the town of Silverhampton".

(Double Thread - 1899)

An 1870's photograph of the Anglo-Saxon pillar in St Peter's churchyard
(Photograph Joyce Perry courtesy St Peter's Church)

Two 1890's photographs of Queen Square showing the old shops Ellen would have known, and also the Empire Music Hall
(Photographs courtesy Wolverhampton Archives and Local Studies)

(b) St Peter's Church, Apse, Lion, Chancel Frescoes

St Peter's Church was obviously well-known to Ellen, both inside and out. Although brought up in Methodism, she later became a member of the Church of England. George Thorneycroft had been a churchwarden at St Peter's, and gave handsomely towards its restoration. He is commemorated by a brass plaque and a stone tablet depicting his head, both of which are attached to the walls inside, and both of which were given by his son Thomas.

"The next day Miss Camilla Desmond took her nephew Jack Le Mesurier all over the 'Old Church' as it is called to distinguish it from all the other and newer churches of the town. She loved every detail of the grand old edifice, down from the beautiful apse at the east end to the quaintly hideous stone creature keeping watch at the foot of the pulpit steps. The frescoes that line the chancel were newer than these, were newer even than Miss Camilla

St Peter's Church in the 1870's looked very little different from today.
(Photograph Joyce Perry courtesy St Peter's Church)

The 15th Century stone lion still guards the pulpit steps (Photograph Joyce Perry courtesy St Peter's Church)

The frescoes were covered many years ago by the plain white of the chancel walls we see today. (Photograph Joyce Perry courtesy St Peter's Church)

herself; but to her they were of the deepest interest, as they had been painted from time to time in memory of the departed friends of her early days, and to look at them was like looking at faded portraits or at packets of old letters. In fact, the 'Old Church' seemed even more home to her than the Deanery, and she loved it even better."

(Double Thread - 1899)

The Drive from the Lich Gate to the South Porch has changed little in a hundred years (Photograph Joyce Perry)

(c) St Peter's Church - East Window

"Elisabeth was silent; she was much too excited to speak. Her heart was thumping like the great hammer at the Osierfield, and she was trembling all over. So she held her peace as they drove up the principal street of Silverhampton and across the King's Square to the lych-gate of St Peter's Church; but Alan, looking into the tell tale face he knew so well, was quite content.

Yet as she sat beside Alan in St Peter's Church that summer evening, and thought upon what she had just done, a great sadness filled Elisabeth's soul. The sun shone brightly through the western window, and wrote mystic messages upon the grey stone walls; but the lights of the east window shone pale and cold in the distant apse, where the Figure of the Crucified gleamed white upon a foundation of emerald. And as she looked at the Figure Which the world has wept over and worshipped for nineteen centuries, she realised that this was the Symbol of all that she was giving up and leaving behind her - the Sign of that

The focal point of this passage is one of a series of windows around the apse by Michael O'Connor and Sons, dating from the reconstruction of the chancel in 1865. (Photograph Joyce Perry courtesy St Peter's Church)

religion of love and sorrow which men call Christianity.

She had never understood before how much that Symbol of eternal love and vicarious suffering had been to her, nor how puzzling would be the path through the wilderness if there were no Crucifix at life's cross-roads to show the traveller which way to go; and her heart grew heavier as she took part in the sacred office of Evensong, and thought how beautiful it all would be if only it were true. She longed to be a little child again - a child to whom the things which are not seen are as the things which are seen, and the things which are not as the things which are; and she could have cried with homesickness when she remembered how firmly she had once believed that the shadow which hung over the Osierfield was a pillar of cloud by day and a pillar of fire by night, to testify that God was still watching over His people, as in the days of old. Now she knew that the pillar was only the smoke and the flame of human industries; and the knowledge brought a load of sadness, as it seemed to typify that there was no longer any help for the world but in itself.

When the Bishop ascended the pulpit, Elisabeth recalled her wandering thoughts and set herself to listen. No one who possesses a drop of Nonconformist blood can ever succeed in not listening to a sermon, even if it be a poor one; and the Bishop of Merchester was one of the finest preachers of his day. His text was, 'Blessed art thou, Simon Bar-jona: for flesh and blood hath not revealed it unto thee;' and he endeavoured to set forth how it is only God Who can teach men about God and how flesh and blood can never show us the Christ until He chooses to reveal Himself. At first Elisabeth listened only with her mind, expecting an intellectual treat and nothing more; but as he went on, and showed how the Call comes in strange places and at strange times, and how when it comes there is no resisting it, her heart began to burn within her; and she recognised the preacher, not only as a man of divers gifts and great powers, but as the ambassador of Christ sent direct to her soul. Then slowly her eyes were opened, and she knew that the Figure in the east window was no Sign of an imaginary renunciation, no Symbol of a worn-out creed, but the picture of a living Person, Whose Voice was calling her, and Whose Love was constraining her, and Whose Power was enfolding her and would not let her go. With the certainty that is too absolute for proof she knew in Whom she now believed; and she knew, further, that it was not her own mind nor the preacher's words that had suddenly shown her the truth - flesh and blood had not revealed it to her, but Christ Himself.

When the service was over, Elisabeth came out into the sunlight with a strange, new, exultant feeling, such as she had never felt before. She stood in the old churchyard, waiting for Alan to bring round the dog-cart, and watching the sun set beyond the distant hills; and she was conscious - how she could not explain - that the sunset was different from any other sunset that she had ever seen. She had always loved nature with an intense love; but now there seemed a richer gold in the parting sunbeams - a sweeter mystery behind the far-off hills - because of that Figure in the east window. It was as if she saw again a land which she had always loved, and now learned for the first time that it belonged to some one who was dear to her; a new sense of ownership mingled with the old delight, and gave an added interest to the smallest detail.

Then she and Alan turned their backs to the sunset, and drove along the bleak high-road towards Sedgehill, where the reflection of the blast-furnaces - that weird aurora borealis of the Black Country - was already beginning to pulsate against the darkening sky. And here again Elisabeth realized that for her the old things had passed away, and all things had become new. She felt that her childish dream was true, and that the crimson light was indeed a pillar of fire showing that the Lord was in the midst of His people; but she went further now than she had gone in her day-dreams, and knew that all the lights and shadows of life are but pillars of cloud and of fire, forthtelling the same truth to all who have seeing eyes and understanding hearts."

(Farringdons - 1900)

(d) The Deanery

"Camilla Desmond lived alone in a square red brick house, which was called The Deanery, in memory of the time when Silverhampton boasted a Dean of its own, and provided him with a local habitation. This house was panelled throughout with black oak, and boasted one of the finest carved staircases in the county. Her father, as his father before him, had been a solicitor of the old school, a very stately and handsome man, who knew all the county families round about, and likewise all their secrets; and his beautiful daughter was often invited to accompany him when he visited the various noblemen and gentry in the neighbourhood. So Camilla knew the county as well as the town and could hold her own with anybody."

(Double Thread - 1899)

The Deanery dated from about 1656, possibly designed by (certainly in the style of) Sir Christopher Wren, whose father and uncle were both Deans of Wolverhampton. It was demolished in the 1920s, despite public protest, to make way for the College of Technology, the present University main building. (Photograph courtesy Wolverhampton Archives and Local Studies)

The Deanery's main staircase. (Photograph courtesy Wolverhampton Archives and Local Studies)

(e) Iron Manufacture and Blast Furnaces

George Thorneycroft and his brother Edward began as ordinary ironworkers, and through hard work and skill eventually became the largest employers of labour in Wolverhampton. Their partnership at the Shrubbery Ironworks, Horseley Fields, began in 1824, and though they became wealthy, they were noted for paying their workers above the average wage.

"The staple commodity of the citizens of this place is iron, which they manufacture and buy and sell; and the iron gets into their blood, and makes strong men of them. Sometimes it happens that the iron turns into gold which is good; but the danger is that this may get into their blood too, and so cause them to lose their sense of perspective in this world, and their view of the next altogether."

(Double Thread - 1899)

(f) The Osier Bed Works, Lower Horseley Fields

"In the dark valley lying to the immediate edge of Sedgehill stood the Osierfield Works, the largest ironworks in Mershire in the good old days when Mershire made iron for half the world. The owners of these works were the Farringdons, and had been so for several generations. So it came to pass that the Farringdons were the royal family of Sedgehill; and the Osierfield Works was the circle wherein the inhabitants of that place lived and moved. It was as natural for everybody born in Sedgehill eventually to work at the Osierfield as it was for him eventually to grow into a man and to take unto himself a wife."

(The Farringdons - 1900)

(g) Royal Hospital

The Royal Hospital was an institution to which George Thorneycroft gave money, when funds were needed for setting up the hospital.

"When they arrived at Silverhampton hospital Rufus Webb's sun had well-nigh gone down. But he knew Michael, and evinced a wish to speak to him alone; so the doctor went away leaving the two together.

'I am so thankful you have come' the sick man gasped; 'I was afraid you would not arrive in time, and I cannot die in peace until I have extracted a promise from you to do something for me after I am gone.'

(Fuel of Fire - 1902)

An early photograph when the building was referred to as The General Hospital.
(Photograph courtesy Wolverhampton Archives and Local Studies)

(h) Compton Road

"It was on an Easter morning, somewhere about the middle of the nineteenth century, that Tertius Clayton thus attacked the great Festival which the Church was then celebrating; and it was on the high-road leading from the town of Silverhampton to the village of Crompton that the attack took place. In those days Silverhampton had not yet thoroughly awaked from sleep, nor stretched out her long arms in the direction of Tetleigh and Crompton and Fenn and Sedgehill, as she does at the present time, until all these outlying districts have become almost a part of herself. Instead, a perfect wilderness of orchards made a complete hiatus between the town and the villages surrounding her - orchards which were alike a wonder of beauty, whether covered with snow-drifts of white blossoms, or crowned with golden coronets of ripened fruit."

(Place and Power - 1903)

(i) The House That Jack Built, Compton Road

"Mr Clayton's home, rejoicing in the singular name of The House That Jack Built (though why and wherefore nobody knew) was an old, white, substantial house at the beginning of the road which led from Silverhampton to Northbridge. Now the old house is in a street of buildings of later growth: but in those days it was considered quite a country residence; and there was a toll-gate between it and Silverhampton, where the dusty wayfarer might slake his thirst in curds and whey."

(Place and Power - 1903)

An early 1900s photograph of Compton Road, with the Royal Oak public house on the left, and on the extreme right the house which was in real life called The House That Jack Built. (Photograph courtesy Wolverhampton Archives and Local Studies)

(j) Horsehills, off Richmond Road

"Josiah's three sisters, Jemima, Kezia, and Keren-happuch, stayed on in their father's home - a square white house standing some little way off the high-road which leads from Silverhampton to Northbridge. Although it was situated barely two miles from the market-place, Oxhills, as the house was called, was in the depth of the country. Between it and the town stretched that wonderful wilderness of orchards; and on the other side the lonely road dipped down between natural walls of red sandstone, until it crossed the canal at the foot of the hill, and ascended the steep Holloway beyond".

(Place and Power - 1903)

Oxhills was in real life Horsehills, where Horsehills Drive now stands off Richmond Road.
It was the early home of Sir Rowland Hill.
(Photograph courtesy Wolverhampton Archives and Local Studies by permission of the Express and Star)

(k) Chapel Ash Farm

"Conrad took Griselda to Switzerland after their marriage, and then brought her home to a charming old house which he had, to his great delight, succeeded in securing. It was a square house, of that rich red Mershire brick which in time becomes a lovely rose colour, situated on an eminence between the Tetleigh and the Crompton Roads, about a mile and a half from the town. On the one side its meadows sloped down to the canal at Tetleigh, and on the other to the garden behind the Stillingfleets' house, so that Griselda and Lois could interchange visits without going outside their own domains at all".

(Place and Power - 1903)

Chapel Ash Farm as it was in 1916. Much of its farm land is now covered by St. Peter's and St Edmund's Schools, and University and Wulfrun College property.
(Photograph courtesy Wolverhampton Archives and Local Studies)

(l) Tettenhall Road

"In the afternoon Miss Camilla and Jack drove to the pretty village of Tetleigh, about two miles west of Silverhampton. They passed by rows of houses and streets of villas, where there had been nothing but apple-orchards when Miss Camilla was a girl; and the town did not actually come to a full stop till they crossed the canal, which lay like a river at the foot of the hill."

(Double Thread - 1899)

An early 1900s photograph of the villas in Tettenhall Road, the location of which can still be easily recognised. (Photograph courtesy Wolverhampton Archives and Local Studies)

(m) House at Compton Road

"Lois was the only child of Stephen Ireby, the leading book seller in Silverhampton. For four generations the Irebys had kept the old book shop in King's Square, until they had grown as proud of it as men grow of a landed estate. For four generations they had proved themselves gentlemen in the true sense of the word, doing justly and loving mercy and walking humbly with their God; and they had, moreover, read and re-read the books by which they were surrounded, until they became one of the most cultured families in Mershire.

Stephen no longer lived over the shop, as his fathers had done before him; for the sake of his motherless child he had taken a house in the country - a small, red, sunny house, standing on a steep incline which overhung the Crompton Road, about a quarter of a mile from Oxhills; and there little Lois had thriven as she never would have thriven in the town".

(Place and Power - 1903)

This seems the most likely candidate for Stephen Ireby's house, overhanging Compton Road. (Photograph courtesy Wolverhampton Archives and Local Studies)

(n) Dunstall Hall

"Shortly after his father's death, Laurence took his degree. Meanwhile his mother had gone to her brother, Lord Portcullis (whose wife had recently died), and had taken charge of his household at Drawbridge Castle. As a tutor was required to teach the rising Drawbridge how to shoot, it occurred to the heads of the family that Laurence Baxendale might take the post. He was not specially attracted by the prospect; but his pockets were so empty that there was room in them for his inclinations as well as his salary; so he was compelled to pocket both"

(Fuel of Fire - 1902)

Traditionally Dunstall Hall had been the home of Lady Wulfrun.
Its successor, a moated mansion, was demolished in the 1920s to make way for Courtauld's textile factory, and the area is now covered by works, the race course and part of Farndale Housing Estate.
(Photograph courtesy Wolverhampton Archives and Local Studies)

Tettenhall

(a) Tettenhall Church and Churchyard

St Michael and All Angels' Church, Tettenhall, was where Ellen married schoolmaster Alfred Felkin on 16 April 1903. The service was conducted by Reverend William Robert Hamilton, who in the same year was wed himself, to Ellen's sister Edith. The churchyard was where members of the Thorneycroft family were buried. Next to some of the graves at the top of the bank in the south-western corner of the churchyard was also where Ellen's father and mother were buried. Her mother died on 6 January 1911, and was buried on the 11th. Her father did not recover from this, being already frail, and died on 25 February. His funeral was on 1 March, taken by the Bishop of Lichfield.

"When they reached Tetleigh, Miss Camilla insisted on Jack's getting out of the carriage and seeing the beautiful old church there, as old, if not older, than the one in Silverhampton, though Jack was lazy and would fain have stayed where he was. And then she marched him through one of the most picturesque churchyards in Mershire, and showed him a very

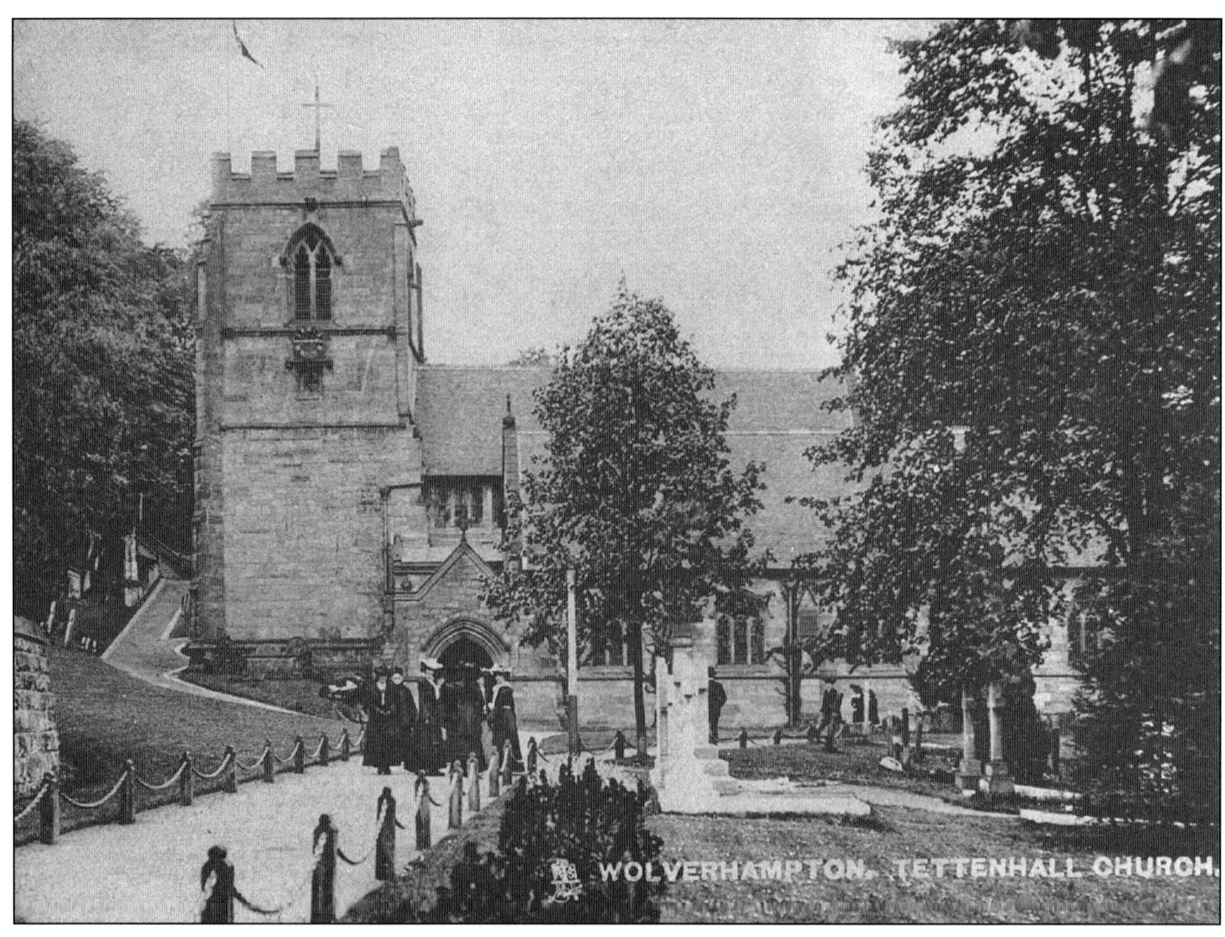

St Michael and All Angels was a major mediaeval church, as shown in this turn of the century photograph. Much of it had to be rebuilt after a fire in 1950. (Photograph courtesy Wolverhampton Archives and Local Studies)

A view of the churchyard showing the Thorneycroft tombs at the top of the bank. (Photograph courtesy Wolverhampton Archives and Local Studies)

ancient monument representing a woman without arms or legs, which was one of the curiosities of the neighbourhood.

'The story runs' she exclaimed, 'that this woman sewed on a Sunday and at last her parish priest heard of it, and forbade her to do so any more. She promised him she would not do so, and he went away. But the very next Sunday she drew a curtain over the window, so that no one could see her, and went on sewing as usual. The priest knew that she had disobeyed him, and he went to her again; but she swore a great oath that she had not, and she uttered a blasphemous prayer that her arms and legs might drop off if she ever sewed on a Sunday again'. Miss Camilla stopped in her walk along the avenue of lime-trees and said solemnly: 'In spite of the priest's continued warnings, the woman continued to sew on a Sunday, and so her arms and legs dropped off as she had said.'"

(Double Thread 1899)

(b) Tettenhall Vicarage

"When the vicar and his wife were sitting at breakfast in the vicarage one morning, not long after their return to Tetleigh, the maid brought in the card of Dr Arrowsmith, one of the Silverhampton doctors.

"What on the earth can he want?' said Michael, looking at the card.

'Let's have him in and ask him,' Nora suggested; 'it will be the simplest way of finding out; just as opening one's letters is so much simpler than trying to guess from the post-mark who they come from - yet nearly everybody tries the latter method first.'"

(Fuel of Fire - 1902)

(c) House on Old Hill

"Jack puffed silently at his pipe, and the rector, Philip Cartwright, continued: 'I was born at Tetleigh, a village about two miles from Silverhampton, and the sweetest village in the whole world'.

'I know it,' said Jack shortly. Silverhampton was too redolent of memories of Ethel to be a pleasing subject of conversation to him just then.

A late Victorian photograph of the steep old hill with Philip Cartwright's house half way up on the left.
(Photograph courtesy Wolverhampton Archives and Local Studies)

'Then you know the nicest place on this earth and the prettiest. Well, if you know Tetleigh, you know the Old Hill; that steep hill up which the coaches had to crawl on all fours before the new road was cut right through the sandstone some sixty years ago, but which is now too steep for vehicles. And you know a dear old house, built on so steep a slope of the hill that upstairs is downstairs and downstairs is upstairs, as in *De Quincey's Dream of Jean Paul Richter*. The front-door has a reserved and dignified aspect as all right-minded front-doors are bound to have which open right on the street with no gardens to chaperone them; but the back of the house belies its stern exterior, and is gay and bright and sunny, with tiers of grassy little terraces commanding a fine view of Silverhampton, which is a city set on a hill. And the terraces all come to an untimely end in a little wood, where you will find in the spring the bluest bluebells that are to be found in England. There are none bluer anywhere, and to my mind, none half so sweet. That is the house where I was born."

(Double Thread - 1899)

(d) House at High Street

"Philip Cartwright continued, speaking more to himself than to Jack: 'At the top of the Old Hill there is another dear old house, but after a different fashion; a house which is surrounded by a high garden-wall, and so never has to be on its dignity; just as women, who have always been guarded and sheltered, are more gracious than those who are obliged to fight life's battles for themselves. This old house has a garden chock-full of sunshine; and when you open the green garden-door, some of the sunshine overflows, and lies in a big

Upper Green / High Street, where part of Laura Greenfield's house is just visible on the extreme right. This was Tettenhall Police Station, and a shopping arcade now stands on the site (Photograph courtesy Wolverhampton Archives and Local Studies)

splash right across Tetleigh High Street. I have often seen it happen. And there is an old sun-dial in the midst of the garden to mark the sunny hours; and all the sunny hours of my life have been noted there; for that old house was once the home of Laura Greenfield, and Laura Greenfield was the only woman in this world or the next for me.'"

(Double Thread - 1899)

(e) The Rock

"That was in the days before the new road had been cut right through the solid red sandstone of Tetleigh Rock, in order to shorten the journey of the mail-coaches from the Midlands to the Western Sea. Nowadays the old high-road is silent and untrodden save by the feet of workmen going to and from their work in the fields, and of lovers mistaking its grassy pathway for the main-line to fairyland."

(Place and Power - 1903)

Trams would certainly not have reached Tettenhall village if the Rock had not been cut through in the 1820s by Telford as part of his improvements to the Holyhead route.
(Photograph courtesy Wolverhampton Archives and Local Studies)

(f) Tettenhall Towers

Tettenhall Towers became the home of George Thorneycroft's only surviving son Thomas in 1851. The house is said to have originated as an inn called the Holly Bush, partly demolished and rebuilt in the 18th Century. The Thorneycrofts proceeded to double the size of the house, with one of its principal features being a Great Hall, or theatre/ballroom, with a stage, gallery, ornate fireplace and Colonel Thorneycroft's patent sprung dance floor, one his many inventions. Other inventions were sanitary, such as devices to ventilate drains and draw off sewer gas, and domestic, with a lift, telegraphic communication and signalling equipment installed in the house.

Colonel Thorneycroft and carriage party pose in the drive of Tettenhall Towers. (Photograph courtesy Wolverhampton Archives and Local Studies)

A rear view of Tettenhall Towers. (Photograph courtesy Wolverhampton Archives and Local Studies)

Colonel Thorneycroft's magnificent ballroom / theatre with gallery and ornate chimney piece. (Photograph courtesy Wolverhampton Archives and Local Studies)

"About two miles to the west of Silverhampton stood Tetleigh Towers, the country seat of Sir Conrad Clayton. The house was one of those fascinating edifices which, after the manner of the immortal Topsy, had not been built but had 'growed'; a large, delightful, rambling mansion, full of charming surprises, where nothing existed save the unexpected. There was an ideal country drawing-room on one side of the hall - a long, low, sunny room made still sunnier by plentiful white paint and a pale blue carpet and curtains; and an ideal dining-room on the other side - a room of mysterious nooks and corners, rendered still more mysterious by furniture and panellings of finely carved black oak; and then where the house ought to have ended according to all laws of domestic architecture- where, in fact, any house would have ended that had a spark of conventionality in its composition - there came a conservatory of orange-trees and marble fountains, leading into the finest ballroom in all Mershire, with two galleries running round it, and a huge chimney-corner big enough to roast an ox; and beyond that came billiard-rooms and smoking-rooms and gun-rooms galore. Certainly there never was such a house for surprises as Tetleigh Towers!"

(Place and Power - 1903)

(g) View from Tettenhall Towers

"On the other side of the valley Silverhampton lay asleep in the afternoon sunshine. Because it was a holiday and because the wind was in the west, there was hardly any smoke in the air; and so the tower of St Peter's Church stood out on the crest of the hill against the blue sky with clear and unblurred outlines. Further along the ridge came Sedgehill Church and Sedgehill Beacon, likewise pointing heavenwards - as indeed all things point at Eastertide, be they grey church towers or flowers of the field."

(Place and Power - 1903)

(h) Gorsty Hayes

"It fell upon a day (so the ancient chronicles tell us) before men had discovered that Mershire was a land whose stones were of iron and her foundations of coal, that Guy, the eldest son of Sir Stephen de Baxendale, went out hunting in the merry greenwood which lay between Baxdendale Hall and Silverhampton town. And because Guy was too young to take such heed to his own steps and the steps of his steed, as an older and wiser huntsman would have done, the horse put his foot into a rabbit-hole, thereby bringing himself and his rider to the ground. In much fear and trembling the retainers picked up the unconscious form of their young master and bore him to Gorsty Hayes, a forester's lodge in the heart of the wood, which is standing to this day. There he was nursed back to consciousness by Vivien of the Glade, the forester's fair daughter, much famed in those parts for her skill in discovering healing herbs and distilling soothing potions from the same."

(Fuel of Fire - 1902)

The seventeenth century Gorsty Hayes Cottage stands at the edge of what used to be known as Kingsley Wood. This was owned by the Thorneycroft family from the late nineteenth century onwards.
(Photograph courtesy Wolverhampton Archives and Local Studies)

(i) Woodthorne

Woodthorne was Ellen's own home, from the age of seven until she married in 1903. It was built by her father for the family in 1867, and remained his home until he and his wife passed away in 1911. The Ministry of Agriculture Fisheries and Foods took it over in 1946 and demolished the house some twenty years ago to make way for new offices.

"It was a summer's afternoon and Anthony and his cousins were sitting in the garden of Wayside, the Burtons' house, about three miles from the manufacturing town of Silverhampton. Mr Burton, the girls' father, was an iron master, as his father had been before him; and he and Anthony drove every day to the Works in the dark valley on the other side of the ridge which divides, as by a straight line, the Black Country of the Midlands from the woods and hills and meadowlands of West Mershire.

Wayside was a red-brick house on the high road leading from Silverhampton to Salopshire and thence to the western sea. It was approached from the road by a long solemn drive, bordered by specimen shrubs which Nancy said had a depressing appearance, because evergreens always gave her the blues; but the house itself was cheerful and comfortable enough; and the garden at the back faded away into fields which in their turn ended in some of the prettiest lanes in England. As a child Nancy thought these lanes led straight into fairyland; as a woman she knew that they did; but this fuller knowledge only came after she had trodden those green and mysterious ways in company with the man of her choice - and sundry others."

(Fuel of Fire - 1902)

Wayside was Ellen Thorneycroft Fowler's own home, Woodthorne.
(Photograph courtesy Wolverhampton Archives and Local Studies)

(j) The Wergs and Codsall

"The Ways was probably so called because five ways met there: one went eastward past the Burton's house, and through the pretty village of Tetleigh straight to Silverhampton; another took the opposite direction, and led the traveller, by the hills of Salopshire and Wales, to the coast of the western sea; a third went northward down a shady lane, past Ways Hall, the home of the Fairfax family, to Codswell - a picturesque village whose cobble-paved street climbed bravely up a church-crowned hill, which stood as high as Baxendale or Silverhampton; a fourth lay through the well-wooded glades of Baxendale Park, and finally, by slow ascents, reached the Hall itself; and the fifth went due south into a green maze of lanes, which wandered on and on until they finally lost themselves in fairyland - as English lanes have a habit of doing, if only they are taken in the right way.

The spot where these five ways met was marked by a group of fine old elm-trees, growing upon a grassy mound; and round about it were clustered a farm or two and sundry cottages, a picturesque post-office and a blacksmith's forge. It was a pretty hamlet in the typically English style; and its quaint little inn, The Crown, slumbered in a cosy bed of blossom, with a coverlet of climbing roses."

(Fuel of Fire - 1902)

The view up the cobbled street to Codsall church.
(Photograph courtesy Wolverhampton Archives and Local Studies)

(k) Wergs Hall

Wergs Hall was rebuilt in an Italianate style in 1852, with grounds containing a lake and trout stream. The estate was sold off in parcels in 1872, and the purchaser of the Hall was Thomas Perry, Bilston ironmaster. On his death in 1885 he left the property to his brother Frederick Charles Perry, who had married George Thorneycroft's daughter Harriet in 1850. Frederick Perry's sister Helen lived at the Hall until her death in 1907.

"Ways Hall was a long, low, white house, clothed with Virginia Creeper, which made it as a green bower in summer, while in autumn it appeared as a house which was enveloped by crimson flame, and yet not consumed. It was set in the centre of velvet lawns which - like the famous lawns of Oxford - had been rolled for five hundred years, and which sloped down to a large sheet of water inhabited and defended to the best of their ability - by a family of swans. The banks of this lake were covered every spring with daffodils and periwinkles, which looked at their reflection in the water and danced with pleasure at the sight. At least the daffodils did; the periwinkles only nodded and said to themselves, 'What pretty blue eyes we have!'"

(Fuel of Fire - 1902)

Wergs Hall and gardens.
(Photograph courtesy Wolverhampton Archives and Local Studies)

Wergs Hall Lake.
(Photograph courtesy Wolverhampton Archives and Local Studies)

(l) The Red House

"Somewhere in the middle of the maze of lanes which lay between The Ways and Tetleigh Wood stood an old, red farmhouse, sentinelled by a row of poplar-trees. From its front windows one could see the stretch of green fields that lay between it and the wood, and beyond them the distant mountains which hid from the casual observer the wonderful doings of the setting sun; and from its back windows one could see Baxendale Hall, standing on the top of a green hill and supported by regiments of trees on either side.

It was at this old, red house - called Poplar Farm - that Laurence and his mother took up their abode when the second marriage of Lord Portcullis made that nobleman's castle too full (and some people said too warm) to hold them. It belonged to them, being situated on the Baxendale property; and, though small, was quite as large an abode as their very limited means permitted."

(Fuel of Fire - 1902)

(m) Wrottesley Hall

The Hall was rebuilt in 1696 By Sir Walter Wrottesley. It was gutted by fire in 1897 and remained derelict until 1923 when the Fourth Lord Wrottesley built a smaller house on the same foundations and using a lot of the materials from the old one. The old house had been home to the previous Lord Wrottesley, whose daughter Evelyn was to marry Sir Henry Fowler's son Henry Ernest in 1910. Both fathers were quite elderly and frail when they attended the wedding, and within a few months both had passed away.

"Baxendale Hall, which was built for the third time - having been twice destroyed by fire - in the reign of James the Second, was a fine, square house of red brick, with stone facings. It stood in the centre of an undulating park, on the borders of Mershire and Salopshire, about a mile from a small hamlet known as The Ways; and the house was situated upon such an eminence that its cellars were on a line with the tower of Silverhampton Church. Thus Silverhampton Church and Baxendale Hall looked at each other, from their respective hills, across a fruitful and well-populated valley - a pleasant land of meadows and orchards and comfortable houses, made happy by the money that was coined in the murky coal-fields on the other side of the town."

(Fuel of Fire - 1902)

Sir Walter Wrottesley's grand mansion.
(Photograph courtesy Wolverhampton Archives and Local Studies)

(n) Wrottesley Hall Interior

"The most interesting feature of the house was a large library, filled with all manner of rare old books and fine pictures, and containing many priceless manuscripts and valuable prints. It occupied the whole length of the front of the house upon the first floor, and was exactly over the great entrance hall. Behind it, and over the reception rooms, was the suite of rooms always occupied by the master and mistress of the house; and next to these the nurseries and schoolroom, where generations of little Baxendales had played their games and learned their lessons. The guest-chambers were in one wing of the house, over the justice-room and the muniment -room, and the rooms where the men smoked, played billiards and managed the estate; the opposite wing was devoted to the kitchens and offices, and over them were the servants' apartments. The front of the Hall looked east, to where the old churches of Silverhampton and Sedgehill stood as landmarks to the surrounding country; and the gardens at the back borrowed much of their glory from the sun which set behind the distant Welsh hills."

(Fuel of Fire 1902)

Wrottesley Hall after the disastrous fire in 1897.
(Photograph courtesy Wolverhampton Archives and Local Studies)

o) Wrottesley Hall as Rebuilt

"A new house now stands on the site of old Baxendale Hall - a picturesque, red-brick house, designed after the fashion of the Elizabethans, but with every modern comfort and convenience. It smiles across the valley at Silverhampton Church on the opposite hill, as its three predecessors smiled before it; but now there is no shadow on its smile - no shadow of a curse as yet unfulfilled."

(Fuel of Fire - 1902)

Wrottesley Hall following the rebuilding in 1923.
(Photograph courtesy Wolverhampton Archives and Local Studies by permission of Mrs Eisenhofer)

(p) White Gabled House, Tettenhall Wood

"Rufus Webb, for whom Faith had designed her flowers lived alone in a little white - gabled house in the lanes leading from The Ways to fairyland; but the gates of this latter were forever closed to him"

(Fuel of Fire - 1902)

(q) Tettenhall Wood

"Every afternoon Miss Camilla took Jack and Ethel for a drive, for the drives are many and beautiful in that part of Mershire. They drove along Tetleigh Wood, where one can see the whole panorama of three counties spread out before one, and where surely the sun takes more trouble to set becomingly as he takes anywhere else; and thence down into the Holloway, and beside the canal, which looks more like a natural river devoted to pleasure than an artificial water-road for the carrying of coal."

(Double Thread - 1899)

An attractive view, at the top of Compton Holloway, of how Tettenhall Wood used to be. (Photograph courtesy Wolverhampton Archives and Local Studies)

(r) View from Compton Holloway

"As Conrad Clayton made this statement of his life's aim and object, he and his father had just reached the top of Crompton Holloway; and they stood still for a moment and looked back at the way they had come, and at the waves and billows of blossoms which filled the valley between them and the town. On the summit of the opposing ridge the towers of the two old churches of Sedgehill and Silverhampton raised their hoary heads to heaven, in silent protest against the philosophy of life thus enunciated by the younger man, and as witnesses to those eternal truths which he and his father had set themselves to refute; and as Conrad hurled his defiance at any Power Which should dare to stand between him and the fulfilment of his ambitions, an answer came to his challenge in the clashing of the Easter bells."

(Place and Power 1903)

The lower end of Compton Holloway.
(Photograph courtesy Wolverhampton Archives and Local Studies)

(s) View from Clive, Pattingham

"It was on one of those bright September mornings when summer comes back just to say goodbye to us once again, that Conrad went out walking, with his gun in his hand, into that far country, belonging to his father which lay between the Northbridge Road and the road to Mattingham. To anyone who had eyes to see, the view from that strip of land must have brought a message too great and too wonderful to be translated into words. The ground sloped down in a sudden descent like an emerald waterfall, and then spread itself out into waves and billows of greensward, until it reached the bottom of the valley, where there lay a perfect garden of orchards and meadows and russet-tinted woods. Through this valley a silver thread marked the high-way which the river had made for itself; and on the other side, in the far blue distance, were ranged the ramparts of the everlasting hills."

The public footpath from The Clive, Pattingham, allows a view similar to what Conrad saw. To the south is the sudden steep slope and view towards Seisdon. (Photograph Joyce Perry)

To the west the undulating ground gradually descends to the Severn Valley, with Brown Clee in the distance. (Photograph Joyce Perry)

Sedgley

(a) High Street

"In the middle of Sedgehill, which is in the middle of Mershire, which is in the middle of England, there lies a narrow ridge of high table-land, dividing, as by a straight line, the collieries and ironworks of the great coal district from the green and pleasant scenery of the western Midlands. Along the summit of this ridge runs the High Street of the bleak little town of Sedgehill; so that the houses on the east side of this street see nothing through their back windows save the huge slag-mounds and blazing furnaces and tall chimneys of the weird and terrible, yet withal fascinating, Black Country; while the houses on the west side of the street have sunny gardens and fruitful orchards, sloping down towards a fertile land of woods and streams and meadows, bounded in the far distance by the Clee Hills and the Wrekin, and in the farthest distance of all by the blue Welsh mountains."

(The Farringdons - 1900)

An early twentieth century view of Sedgley Bull Ring.
(Photograph courtesy Wolverhampton Archives and Local Studies)

(b) Sedgley Methodist Chapel and Stained Glass Window

"Every Sunday Elisabeth accompanied her cousins to East Lane Chapel, at the other end of Sedgehill, and here she saw strange visions and dreamed strange dreams. The distinguishing feature of this sanctuary was a sort of reredos in oils, in memory of a dead and gone Farringdon, which depicted a gigantic urn, surrounded by a forest of cypress, through the shades whereof flitted 'young-eyed cherubins' with dirty wings and bilious complexions, these last-mentioned blemishes being, it is fair to add, the fault of the atmosphere and not of the artist. For years Elisabeth firmly believed that this altar-piece was a trustworthy representation of heaven; and she felt, therefore, a pleasant, proprietary interest in it, as the view of an estate to which she would one day succeed.

There was also a stained-glass window in East Lane Chapel, given by the widow of a leading official. The baptismal name of the deceased had been Jacob; and the window showed forth Jacob's Dream, as a delicate compliment to the departed. Elisabeth delighted in this window, it was so realistic. The patriarch lay asleep, with his head on a little white tombstone at the foot of a solid oak staircase, which was covered with a red carpet neatly fastened down by brass rods; while up and down this staircase strolled fair-haired angels in long white night-gowns and purple wings.

Could the only stained glass window in the building, dating from 1940 and in memory of a church official, be a replacement for the one which Ellen described? (Photograph Joyce Perry)

Tipton Street Methodist Church, built in 1857 and larger than the chapel in Bilston Street is the more likely setting envisaged by Ellen in "The Farringdons". (Photograph Joyce Perry)

The great day in East Lane Chapel was the Sunday School anniversary; and in Elisabeth's childish eyes this was a feast compared with which Christmas and Easter sank to the level of black-letter days. On these festivals the Sunday School scholars sat all together in those parts of the gallery adjacent to the organ, the girls wearing white frocks and blue neckerchiefs, and the boys black suits and blue ties. The pews were strewn with white hymn-sheets, which lay all over the chapel like snow in Salmon, and which contained special spiritual songs more stirring in their character than the contents of the hymn-book; these the Sunday School children sang by themselves, while the congregation sat swaying to and fro to the tune. And Elisabeth's soul was uplifted within her as she listened to the children's voices; for she felt that mystical hush which - let us hope - comes to us all at some time or other, when we hide our faces in our mantles and feel that a Presence is passing by; and is passing by so near to us that we have only to stretch out our hands in order to touch It."

(The Farringdons - 1900)

(c) Bleak House, Dudley Road

"When Elisabeth appeared upon the scene, and subsequently grew up sufficiently to require a playfellow, she found Christopher Thornley ready to hand. He lived with his bachelor uncle in a square red house on the east side of Sedgehill High Street, exactly opposite to the Farringdons' lodge. It was one of those big, bald houses with unblinking windows, that stare at you as if they had not any eyebrows or eyelashes; and there was not even a strip of greenery between it and the High Street. So to prevent the passers-by from looking in and the occupants from looking out, the lower half of each front window was covered with a sort of black crape mask, which put even the sunbeams into half-mourning."

(The Farringdons - 1900)

Bleak House, the home of Christopher Thornley and his uncle, was in real life a doctor's house and Welfare Centre. It stood on Dudley Road between Sedgley and Upper Gornal, not far from the Leopard public house. (Photograph courtesy Dudley Archives and Local History Service)

(d) Cottage West Side of High Street

"The Batesons lived in a clean little cottage on the west side of the High Street, and enjoyed a large garden to the rereward. It was a singular fact that whereas all their windows looked upon nothing more interesting than the smokier side of the bleak and narrow street, their pigsties commanded a view such as can rarely be surpassed for beauty and extent in England. But Mrs Bateson called her front view 'lively' and her back view 'dull', and congratulated herself daily upon the aspect and the prospect of her dwelling-place. The good lady's ideas as to what constitutes beauty in furniture were by no means behind her opinions as to what is effective in scenery. Her kitchen was paved with bright red tiles, which made one feel as if one were walking across a coral reef, and was flanked on one side with a black oak dresser of unnumbered years, covered with a brave array of blue-and-white pottery. An artist would have revelled in this kitchen, with its delicious effects in red and blue; but Mrs Bateson accounted it as nothing. Her pride was centred in her parlour and its mural decorations, which consisted principally of a large and varied assortment of funeral-cards, neatly framed and glazed. In addition to these there was a collection of family portraits in daguerreotype, including an interesting representation of Mrs Bateson's parents sitting side by side in two straight-backed chairs, with their whole family twining around them - a sort of Swiss Family Laocoon; and a picture of Mr Bateson - in the attitude of Juliet and the attire of a local preacher - leaning over a balcony, which was overgrown with a semi-tropical luxuriance of artificial ivy, and which was obviously too frail to support him. But the masterpiece in Mrs Bateson's art-gallery was a soul-stirring illustration of the death of the revered John Wesley. This picture was divided into two compartments: the first represented the room at Wesley's house in City Road, with the assembled survivors of the great man's family weeping round his bed; and the second depicted the departing saint flying across Bunhill Fields' burying-ground in his wig and gown and bands, supported on either side by a stalwart angel."

(The Farringdons - 1900)

(e) Sedgley, Gospel End, Penn Common and Baggeridge

"Sedgehill High Street is nothing but a part of the great high road which leads from Silverhampton to Studley and Slipton and the other towns of the Black Country; but it calls itself Sedgehill High Street as it passes through the place, and so identifies itself with its environment, after the manner of caterpillars and polar bears and other similarly wise and adaptable beings. At the point where this road adopts the pseudonym of the High Street, close by Sedgehill Church, a lane branches off from it at right angles, and runs down a steep slope until it comes to a place where it evidently experiences a difference of opinion as to which is the better course to pursue - an experience not confined to lanes. But in this respect lanes are happier than men and women, in that they are able to pursue both courses, and so learn for themselves which is the wiser one, as is the case with this particular lane. One course leads headlong down another steep hill - so steep that unwary travellers usually descend from their carriages to walk up or down it, and thus are enabled to ensure relief to their horses and a chill to themselves at the same time; for it is hot work walking up or down that sunny precipice, and the cold winds of Mershire await one with equal gusto at the top and at the bottom. At the foot of the hill stretches a breezy common, wide enough to make one think 'long, long thoughts'; and if the traveller looks backward when he has crossed this

A peaceful scene at Gospel End Common.
(Photograph courtesy Wolverhampton Archives and Local Studies)

A stroll in Baggeridge Woods.
(Photograph courtesy Wolverhampton Archives and Local Studies)

common, he will see Sedgehill Church, crowning and commanding the vast expanse, and pointing heavenward with its slender spire to remind him, and all other wayfaring men, that the beauty of this present world is only an earnest and a foretaste of something infinitely fairer.

The second course of the irresolute lane is less adventurous, and wanders peacefully through Badgering Woods, a dark and delightful spot, once mysterious enough to be a fitting hiding-place for the age-long slumbers of some sleeping princess. As a matter of fact, so it was; the princess was black but comely, and her name was Coal. There she had slept for a century of centuries, until Prince Iron needed and sought and found her, and awakened her with the noise of his kisses. So now the wood is not asleep any more, but is filled with the tramping of the prince's men. The old people wring their hands and mourn that the former things are passing away, and that Mershire's youthful beauty will soon be forgotten; but the young people laugh and are glad, because they know that life is greater than beauty, and that it is by her black coalfields, and not by her green woodlands, that Mershire will save her people from poverty, and will satisfy her poor with bread."

(The Farringdons - 1900)

(f) Ellowes Hall and Lodge

"The home of the Farringdons was called the Willows, and was separated by a carriage-drive of half a mile from the town. Its lodge stood in the High Street, on the western side; and the drive wandered through a fine old wood, and across an undulating park, till it stopped in front of a large square house built of grey stone. It was a handsome house inside, with wonderful oak staircases and Adam chimney-pieces; and there was an air of great stateliness about it, and of very little luxury. For the Farringdons were a hardy race, whose time was taken up by the making of iron and the saving of souls; and they regarded sofas and easy-chairs in very much the same light as they regarded theatres and strong drink, thereby proving that their spines were as strong as their consciences were stern".

(The Farringdons - 1900)

In the early nineteenth century this was known as Ellers, and was famous for the ornamental gardening of Samuel Fereday who grew highly flavoured fruits in great profusion. This view dates from the end of the nineteenth century. (Photograph courtesy Wolverhampton Archives and Local Studies)

The grand staircase of Ellowes Hall.
(Photograph courtesy Dudley Archives and Local History Service, by permission of Staffordshire Record Office, C/P/14/6/15/9 & 14 and Crown Copyright Royal Commission on the Historical Monuments of England)

The ornate fireplace of Ellowes Hall dining room.
(Photograph courtesy Dudley Archives and Local History Service, by permission of Staffordshire Record Office, C/P/14/6/15/9 & 14 and Crown Copyright Royal Commission on the Historical Monuments of England)

(g) The Wodehouse

"When Elisabeth Farringdon was a girl, the princess was still asleep in the heart of the wood, and no prince had yet attempted to disturb her; and the lane passed through a forest of silence until it came to a dear little brown stream, which, by means of a dam, was turned into a moat, encircling one of the most ancient houses in England. The Moat House had been vacant for some time, as the owner was a delicate man who preferred to live abroad; and great was the interest at Sedgehill when, a year or two after Elisabeth left school, it was reported that a stranger, Alan Tremaine by name, had taken the Moat House for the sake of the hunting, which was very good in that part of Mershire."

(The Farringdons - 1900)

The Moat House is in fact the Wombourne Wodehouse, a beautiful old house with styles of architecture going back several centuries. The gardens and grounds are also attractive, and the view across the lake gives the impression of a moated house. (Photographs Joyce Perry, by kind permission of Mr and Mrs Phillips)

Bridgnorth

View of Bridgnorth
(Photograph Joyce Perry)

"It is true that a city which is set on a hill cannot be hid: and when that city is as beautiful as the old town of Northbridge on the Severn, no one would wish to hide it, even if such a course were possible. People who have seen both, assert that there is a strong likeness between Northbridge and Jerusalem: those of us who have only seen one, are prepared to swear that - whatever it is like or whatever it is unlike - Northbridge, as it flashes on the eye of the traveller when he reaches the summit of the Hermitage Hill on the road from Silverhampton to the West, is one of the fairest visions that was ever vouchsafed to mortal eyes. The town stands on a hill surrounded by hills; and through the intervening valleys the Severn makes its way from its native spring to the Bristol Channel. The hill on which the dear old town is built is so steep that many of the streets are really staircases: and the summit is crowned by a beautiful church, a red-brick grammar-school, and a black-and-white town hall of great antiquity. The church is built of that rose-coloured-stone peculiar to the Midlands, which always looks as if it retained the hue of the many sunrises and sunsets that have glorified it; and it has one of the ornate square towers of those parts; while at the other end of the town there stands a church of later date, with the white sides and pepper-pot top of the Georgian period, but still also picturesque in its own way. In the lower part of the town, close to the river, is the fine black-and-white half-timbered old mansion where Bishop Percy collected his Anecdotes and composed his Reliques: and in the upper

St Mary's Church
Closing the picturesque view along East Castle Street, the Georgian church with the pepper-pot top is St Mary's, rebuilt in 1792 to the design of Thomas Telford, and now Bridgnorth's parish church.
(Photograph (a) courtesy Clive Gwilt (b) Joyce Perry)

part of the town, close to the church, stands the small thatched cottage where Richard Baxter wrote his Saints' Rest, and penned one of the most beautiful hymns that was ever written: all work worth doing, but methinks that the work done in the cottage was the greater work of the two.

St Leonard's Church
The church of rose-coloured stone is surrounded by a cathedral-like close, and now cared for by the Redundant Churches Commission. After extreme damage during the Civil War it was patched up many times before being much rebuilt in the nineteenth century. (Photograph courtesy Clive Gwilt)

At the edge of the town, near the church with the pepper-pot, in a large and beautiful garden there stands a fine red Georgian house: and in this house in the latter half of the last century there dwelt a doctor, by name George Windybank, with his gently bred wife and his three handsome daughters. The house was large and comfortable, and had that stately air of spacious graciousness which is peculiar to the house of the Georgian era. The garden was of the kind that our grandparents called 'hanging' though why it is difficult to say. The 'hanging gardens' of Babylon, we are led to believe, really did hang: but the 'hanging gardens' of our immediate forefathers did nothing of the kind. They merely, so to speak, ran up and down stairs, carpeting their staircase with all manner of trees and shrubs and beautiful flowers. There were layers of Dr Windybank's garden all down the face of the steep cliff, each layer seeming gayer and prettier than its predecessor: until at last they ended in one of the streets of stairs, which ran straight down to the road beside the river.

The view from the windows of the house and from the top layer of the garden was magnificent; and the air was even better, as the west wind came straight across the Welsh mountains from the Irish Sea."

House at East Castle Street
The Windybanks' house stands at the end of East Castle Street. It is L-shaped, and now divided into two houses, the northern part being Georgian, the southern wing added in the late nineteenth century with a lovely well proportioned room which could be used for entertaining and dances, its French windows making the lawned garden an extension of the room. During the early part of this century it was a dentist's house before being divided. The "hanging gardens" are separated from the garden of the house by Castle Walk, a public footpath.
(Photographs Joyce Perry, courtesy Mr & Mrs Kirk)

"The most thrilling moment was reached when the motor had climbed the steep hill leading to the upper part of the old town of Northbridge, and had pulled up at Mrs Windybank's front door. Caroline and the nurse helped Barbara out of the car; and her grandmother, standing at the gate, welcomed her in a loving embrace. As they walked hand-in-hand up the flagged path to the front door, the girl gazed about her with a puzzled look on her face; that face which was now freed from its bandages, and covered instead by a thick gauze veil."

Bishop Percy's House
"Except the Lord build the owse, the labourers therof evail nothing.
Erected by R For 1580"*

This inscription inside the house gives the date of construction, and its first owner, the name being an abbreviation of Richard Forster or Forester, a trader on the river. Local people felt the house to be too pretentious and christened it "Forester's Folly". It has become known as the birthplace in 1729 of Thomas Percy, son of a grocer, educated at the local grammar school and Oxford. His clerical career led him to be chaplain to George III and Bishop of Dromore. He was famous as the compiler of Reliques of Ancient English Poetry first published 1765. (Photograph courtesy Clive Gwilt)

"The historical instinct - which as it happened both her granddaughters had inherited from her - was very strong in Mrs Windybank: to her all old places and old buildings brought a message from the past; a message full of the wisdom of the ages, illuminated by the beauty of far-off days. Together she and her granddaughter visited Bishop Percy's black-and-white mansion near the banks of the river, and refreshed their minds with his Reliques and his Anecdotes, striving to revive in their own minds the wit and the humour of a bygone age: and together they went to the little white cottage near the church, where Richard Baxter penned one of the most beautiful hymns that was ever written; and there endeavoured to refresh their souls in the spiritual atmosphere still enfolding the abode of that most holy man."

Richard Baxter's Cottage
St Leonard's overlooks the small cottage, not now thatched, where a plaque records its association with Richard Baxter.
(Photograph Joyce Perry)

"Most of the ground floor was panelled at The Chevrons, which was the name of Mrs Windybank's house; so called because in each of the spandrels, formed by the pointed arch over the front door, was carved a shield with a chevron upon it - evidently the coat of the original owner. What his name was nobody knew; the years had wiped it out: and what the coat of arms was nobody knew; the weather of some centuries had obliterated all the carving save the chevrons that crossed the shields: but these had remained to give a name to the house long before Dr Windybank bought it; it had been known as The Chevrons for a hundred years and more. The panelling of the entrance-hall and the library was painted white, as it had been long before the Windybanks' time: but the dining-room was lined to the ceiling with oak grown black with age. The drawing-room - a long low room evidently added at least a hundred and fifty years after the house was built - was not lined with wood at all, but was papered in eighteenth-century fashion, with a white watered paper, divided into square panels by means of gilded mouldings and narrow wreaths of many coloured flowers."

"One summer's morning Barbara and her grandmother were sitting sewing in the library at The Chevrons - a room which needed no panelling as it was entirely lined with books. It was the only room on the ground floor, except the surgery, that looked out on to the street; and Mrs Windybank always enjoyed sitting in the old-fashioned bay-window and watching the passers-by. The surgery was never used as a sitting-room, only as a shelter for Miss Windybank's bicycle and the croquet-set and oddments of that kind - because Mrs Windybank vowed that its atmosphere was impregnated with the pain and anxiety and misery of the people who had visited it in the days when her late husband practised as a doctor in Northbridge."

"Just before starting for India, Kinfell went to Northbridge to bid Mrs Windybank and Caroline good-bye. He insisted on spending the night at the old-fashioned inn overlooking the black-and-white town-hall (which town-hall was built on pillars, the market-place being fashioned out of the space below), because he had to leave so early in the morning that he refused to awaken The Chevrons at so unearthly an hour; but he passed a long afternoon and evening in the company of his wife's aunt and grandmother, and afforded them a great deal of innocent happiness in so doing."

(Beauty and Bands - 1920):

High Street
The timber framed building to the right was formerly one of the principal Bridgnorth hotels 'The Castle'. The Town Hall, rebuilt after the Great Fire of 1646, was made up of stone arches, and the materials of an old barn given to the town by Lady Bartue of Wenlock. (Photograph courtesy Clive Gwilt)

Other Settings

(a) Whiteladies Convent

"It came to pass, when Henry VIII was king, that again a Baxendale lost his heart to a daughter of the people. Once more, as of old, his parents interfered between him and the soul that God had given him, for the sake of the glory of their ancient house. And because Richard Baxendale swore that he would marry the girl he loved, though she was only Agnes Tyler, daughter of a wool-merchant in Silverhampton, Agnes was sent to the convent of Greyladies, and there compelled by her father to take the veil: for how could a plain Mercian wool-merchant defy the wishes of the great Sir Wilfred Baxendale?

So Agnes possessed her sweet soul in patience within the thick stone walls of Greyladies, and passed her time in praying for Richard Baxendale, that he might do honour to his knighthood on earth and finally obtain the heavenly crown which is promised to him that overcometh. There, year after year, she watched the daffodils cover the earth, and she thought upon those golden streets through which Richard and she should one day walk together; and she saw the wild hyacinths carpet the woodlands, and thought upon the pavement of sapphire before which Richard and she would one day kneel. She prayed also for his wife and his children; for her love was not of the earth earthy, and there was no thought of self to be found therein. As for the wool-merchant, her father, he commended himself in that he had at the same time pleased God and Sir Wilfred, by taking his daughter from the one in order to give her to the Other; and he felt that he had thereby conferred an obligation upon both of these Powers which neither of them could lightly discharge. It is always so satisfactory to a man when he can serve God and Mammon at once! There was no doubt that the wool-merchant of Silverhampton was an excellent man of business; and there was also no doubt that two of the parties involved - namely himself and Sir Wilfred - were completely satisfied with the arrangement. Whether the Third Power concerned in the transaction concurred in the approval manifested by the other two is a more doubtful matter, and one whereof the chronicler knows nothing; but Will Tyler himself knows all about it by this time, and probably realises at last the disadvantages of a divided service.

When Agnes was safely out of his reach, Richard took to wife the Lady Anne, daughter of the Earl of Mershire; and by her had three fine sons and four fair daughters. But his heart was always in the convent of Greyladies, some five miles from Baxendale Hall.

It was when Sir Richard's hair was thinning and his beard was turning grey that the Reformation altered the whole political aspect of England, and Henry VIII appropriated to himself the religious house of Greyladies and all the properties appertaining thereto. The convent was sacked, and the nuns fled to Baxendale, taking with them as much treasure as they could carry; for Sir Richard, being but a simple English gentleman, could not understand how even kings should rise superior to the Eighth Commandment and yet go unpunished.

The King's soldiers, in the King's name, commanded Sir Richard to give up the treasures of the convent , or else they would burn Baxendale Hall to the ground; but he laughed in their faces, and swore that the nuns who had fled to him for safety should find it there until his death.

Greyladies is the Priory of St Leonard at Brewood, known as White Ladies, founded in the 12th Century for nuns or canonesses of the Order of St Augustine. It was dissolved in 1536, and all that remains are the ruins of the church. Until 1844 it was still a Roman Catholic burial ground. The site is now in the care of English Heritage. (Photograph courtesy Wolverhampton Archives and Local Studies)

Then the King's soldiers, in the King's name , set fire to the Hall. The Lady Anne and her children escaped; but Sir Richard stayed with the nuns whom he was defending, like the brave knight that he was, and perished with them in the final crash.

Tradition says that just at the end - when all hope or chance of life was over, and death was waiting for them both - Sir Richard threw back the veil which for so long had divided him from Agnes, and kissed her once more full upon the lips, as he had been wont to kiss her long ago in the merry greenwood between Baxendale and Silverhampton. If this were so, no one saw it save the God Who made them man and woman before they were knight and nun, and therefore would not go back upon His Own handiwork; and their souls are in His keeping until this day."

(Fuel of Fire -1902)

(b) Tong Church and College

"Another day they went by the old coach-road to Pembruge, the far-famed village of Nell and her grandfather in the Old Curiosity Shop; where the ideal old church is like a miniature cathedral, and stands with its ruined college, close by the edge of a lake bespangled with water-lilies. At the head of the lake is a fantastically devised castle, like the palace in some quaint old fairy-tale; and all the woods around are a veritable queen's garden of wild flowers, and are in turn paved with marble and gold and amethyst, according as it is the season for snowdrops or daffodils or bluebells. It was too late for spring flowers when Jack and Ethel went to Pembruge; but they wandered through the woods and worshipped in the church, and the stone crusaders there seemed to Jack to be repeating the same message that the warriors at Greystone had already brought - that message of the littleness of temporal and the greatness of eternal things."

(Double Thread - 1899)

Tong Church and College
In 1409 Lady Isabel de Pembrugge obtained a licence from King Henry IV to found Tong College, and to build the present church, most of which is therefore the early 15th Century rebuilding in Perpendicular style. The College was seized by Henry VIII in 1546. (Photographs Joyce Perry)

Charles Dickens set the end of The Old Curiosity Shop at Tong, but the grave of Little Nell is fictional, set up as a tourist attraction. (Photograph Joyce Perry)

(c) Tong Castle

John Hartley was a glass manufacturer from Smethwick, who became an ironmaster and partner in the Thorneycroft firm. He married Emma, one of George Thorneycroft's daughters, and after a period at Summerfield, and at 'The Oaks', Merridale Road, Wolverhampton, John and Emma became tenants of Tong Castle, a grand place with turreted roofs and Turkish domes, an unusual mix of Gothic and Moorish styles. It was owned by the Earl of Bradford. After many years of disuse and dereliction this century it was declared dangerous and demolished with dynamite in the 1950's.

"At last they came to a picturesque wall and gateway, built of the red stone which belongs to that part of the country, and which has a trick of growing so much redder at evening-time that it looks as if the cold stone were blushing with pleasure at being kissed good-night by the sun; and then through a wood sloping on the left side down to a little stream, which was so busy talking to itself about its own concerns that it had not time to leap and sparkle for the amusement of passers-by; until they drew up in front of a quaint old castle, built of the same stone as the outer walls and gateway.

The family were away from home, so the whole of the castle was at the disposal of Alan and his party, and they had permission to go wherever they liked. The state-rooms were in front of the building and led out of each other, so that when all the doors were open anyone could see right from one end of the castle to the other. Dinner was to be served in the large saloon at the back, built over what was once the courtyard; and while his servants were laying the tables with cold viands which they had brought with them, Alan took his guests through the state-rooms to see the pictures, and endeavoured to carry out his plan of educating them and pointing out to them some of the finer works of art."

(Farringdons - 1900)

Tong Castle
The mediaeval castle passed through the de Pembrugge family and was eventually rebuilt in 1760 by George Durant, whose descendants sold it to the Earl of Bradford.
(Photograph courtesy Wolverhampton Archives and Local Studies)

(d) Boscobel House and Oak Tree

"Miss Camilla also took them to the quaint old house, some seven miles from Silverhampton, where Charles II was once hidden in a hole in the cheese-room, and another time in an oak-tree. They saw the oak, which was by now far too old and decrepit to conceal a commoner, much less a king; and they went down into the hole, one at a time, and wondered what it must feel like to be a fugitive monarch."

(Double Thread - 1899)

(e) Badger Dingle, Brewood, Chillington Cross, and Kinver Edge

"They drove to Otter Dingle, which is as beautiful as the Trossachs, though on a smaller scale; they went to Orewood where King John once held his court; they saw the old cross which marks the spot where a wild panther was slain by a knight - though the knight was at one end of a mile-long avenue and the panther at another - because the arrow was winged with a prayer; they visited Kynaston Edge and saw the caves where strange robber-folk dwelt in bygone days; and they learned that the country which is called black is some of the prettiest country in England, just as the people who are called common are often among the saints of the earth."

(Double Thread -1899)

Badger Dingle

A public footpath from the pretty village of Badger leads down into the picturesque Dingle, once part of the landscaped grounds adjoining the long-since demolished Badger Hall. (Photographs Joyce Perry)

Dean Street leads up into the centre of the ancient village of Brewood. (Photograph Joyce Perry)

Chillington Cross is in a lodge garden on the road from Coven to Brewood, at the end of an avenue leading to Chillington Hall. It marks the spot where, in the late 15th Century, Sir John Giffard shot with bow and arrow an escaped panther which was about to kill a woman and her baby. (Photograph Joyce Perry)

(f) Weston Park

"On the great high-road that runs from London to Chester, straight through the heart of the Midlands, stands the village of Dinglewood.

It is a fine old road, and has seen fine old doings in its time. It has echoed to the tramp of the Roman legions as they thundered forth on their triumphant way; it has watched the knights and ladies of the Middle Ages ride by on their armed steeds and their white palfreys. Hereward the Wake made use of it as he rode home on Mare Swallow after playing the potter; and Charles II found it his friend when he escaped to Boscobel after the battle of Worcester. Now it no longer bears the tread of armies or guides the steps of fugitive kings: it has fallen upon more peaceful and eventful days. Instead of Hereward the Wake seeking the merry greenwood, or Charles fleeing from the Parliamentary hosts, tired huntsmen jog along its grassy edges on wintry evenings, wanting rest after a good day's sport; instead of gay post-chaises with their postilions, or mail-coaches with their smoking teams, hay-carts rumble in summer along its broad white path, and farmers drive in their gigs to and from market; and instead of the clash of arms and the tramp of armies, its silence is now broken by the hideous trumpetings of motor-cars. Other days, other manners - sometimes better, sometimes not so good; a truth which has been well trodden into the old road - called by some the Streetway and by others the Watling Street - which runs from London through the heart of the Midlands straight to the western sea.

The gates of Dinglewood Park opened onto the great high-road; and the Hall was about half a mile from them, being approached by a winding drive which bordered a large sheet of water. The Hall itself was a fine old Jacobean house, built of red brick with stone facings, and was replete with beautiful curios and works of art, as its owner was a lady of great artistic taste: and the gardens were counted among the sights of the Midlands, being thrown open to the public one day a week."

(Miss Fallowfield's Fortune - 1908)

Weston Hall, built in 1671 by Lady Wilbraham, now the home of the Earls of Bradford. This view of the south front was taken before the Victorian stucco was removed in the 1930s to reveal the original red brick. (Photograph courtesy Wolverhampton Archives and Local Studies)

(g) Dunston, near Stafford

Dunston Hall would have been known to Ellen as the home of her aunt and uncle - Harriet Thorneycroft married Charles Perry, of the Bilston firm Thomas Perry and Son. They had lived at Summerfield for a short time after their marriage, then Charles built Dunston Hall, which was later to pass to the Thorneycroft side of the family. It was here that MP Peter Thorneycroft was born.

The Frisbys' house still stands behind its red brick wall close to the main Wolverhampton to Stafford Road. (Photograph Joyce Perry)

This view from near Dunston across the countryside towards Cannock Chase is one of the few which are not marred by the intrusion of the heavy motorway traffic. (Photograph Joyce Perry)

"The Frisbys lived in an old, square, red-brick house, close to the high road leading from Silverhampton to Merchester; from which road it was screened by a red-brick wall almost as high as the house itself. On the other side of the house was a large, old-fashioned garden, terminating in fields which sloped down to the river. Beyond the river was a long ridge of rising ground, covered with woods, and dotted with the grey, pointed spires and red cottage-roofs of picturesque little villages. And beyond this again, forming the horizon-line, was a vast tract of wild uncultivated heather-land known as the Chase.

The village of Meadowford - like its fellow-villages on the other side of the river - boasted a few red-tiled cottages and a grey-spired church; and it also contained in addition to the little vicarage, a large white house belonging to the squire, and a smaller red one which Colonel Frisby had considered himself fortunate to secure. It was one of those typical Midland villages, which hug the road and do not stray far from the highway on either side; and it is well that they do not, as the highway is the only permanent means of transit; the country lanes, though exquisitely lovely in spring and summer, are simply impassable in autumn and winter."

(The Wisdom of Folly - 1910)

The Perry family were responsible for replacing the old small brick chapel of St Leonard by the present grand stone church with tower and steeple in the 1870s.
(Photograph Joyce Perry)

Unidentified Places

There are other places and buildings which Ellen uses in her novels which are supposed to be in the Midlands area, but which the writer has so far been unable to identify, and although ideas have come to mind they cannot be verified. Some of the descriptions of these locations are now given, for readers to come up with their own solutions, and it would be interesting to know if any do so.

Claverley Castle

"Claverley Castle was a fine old mansion in the west midlands. It stood on rising ground, well protected on the east by dense woods, and faced the south-west, offering a magnificent view across the broad valley with its golden fields and green meadows which sloped downwards to the silver river, and then rose again until they lost themselves in the blue haze of the perpetual hills and everlasting mountains in the distant west. A spacious valley, usually calm and tranquil, beautiful with a peaceful quietude and home-like restfulness; and yet made glorious on a summer's evening by sunsets which covered the whole sky with gorgeous colouring, till the clouds themselves appeared as chariots of fire driven before the wings of the wind. Yet at times a westerly gale would sweep across the vale, reminding it that there were still undreamed-of beauties and delights beyond those azure hills, and bearing to the midland plain the strength and the scent of the western sea.

The Castle itself was of great antiquity so far as its central portion was concerned, namely, a magnificent hall, where the retainers of the mediaeval barons were wont to assemble - a hall panelled with oak black with age, decorated with suits of ancient armour, and the superb antlers of many a stately stag. At one end was a dais for my lord's dinner-table; on one side was a huge fireplace, at which an ox might have been roasted whole. Around three sides of the hall ran a gallery, out of which opened the bed-chambers. About this central hall successive lords had built and rebuilt, until Claverley Castle became a huge mansion of divers styles of architecture - the whole producing an effect which, if not aesthetically perfect, was at least extremely picturesque."

(Kate of Kate Hall - 1904)

Chayford

"A quaint old town which had long ago ceased to be anything but picturesque, but which never forgot that it had once been prosperous, as some women never forget that they have once been pretty - a town in which the square, red-brick houses pretended that they were frowning on the streets in front, while they were really smiling on the gardens at the back all the time - a town with an interesting past and a most uneventful present - such was Chayford in the county of Mershire."

"The Fords were the most important people in Chayford, and had been rich merchants there for several generations. Edgar's great-grandfather was a friend of John Wesley's; and the great little man had preached the gospel under the huge cedar on the lawn of Chayford House. Consequently at Chayford Chapel the Fords sat in the farthest-back pew, this being ever considered the most august seat - the Woolsack in fact - of Methodist chapels; and their place in the sanctuary was rendered yet more glorious by a brazen fence, wherefrom dangled a sort of short, red moreen petticoat, which ran all along the top of their pew, and so screened the prayers of the Ford family from the prying and plebeian eyes of the rest of the congregation. Mrs Ford pronounced the 'Open Sesame' at all the Wesleyan bazaars and sale-of-work within a radius of ten miles round Chayford; and on such occasions she was specially introduced to the divine notice by the officiating minister under the pseudonym of 'an handmaid'."

(Concerning Isabel Carnaby - 1898)

Greystone`

"Jack alighted at a little roadside station about three miles from Greystone, and was met by a very smart mail phaeton, and a pair of most unmanageable horses. The driving of this neat turn-out gave him distinct pleasure; as the successful management of the unmanageable is a pastime which never fails to bring joy to the masculine heart.

His way lay along a charming old coach road, with broad grassy margins on either side - a road which had been made in the days of the Romans, when land was not yet sold at so much a yard, like ribbon or tape; and Jack drove along the straight white road at a tremendous rate, and felt that the world was very good.

Following the instructions of the groom, he went straight on for nearly three miles, and then turned - through a massive stone gateway surmounted with the arms of the Le Mesuriers - into a fine park, surrounded by a broad belt of woods, and skirted on one side by a wide river. The drive through the park was fully a mile long, and then they turned a sharp corner and came suddenly upon the house - as fine a specimen of a Tudor mansion as could be found in that part of the country.

Sir Roger Le Mesurier was a bachelor, and lived alone; but he never abated a jot or a tittle of the state which he thought incumbent upon the master of Greystone. The establishment and the gardens were as well kept up as if a large and hospitable family, instead of a lonely old man, were living at the hall. The state drawing-rooms were lighted up with countless candles every night. A new butler once, on being told to light up as usual, inquired what company was coming. 'I am coming', replied his master. For the future the butler decided to do as he was bid, and ask no questions - a not unwise decision for others than butlers".

"Jack duly went to the old church at Greystone and sat in a square pew with a fireplace in it, like a cosy little parlour, and looked out on the world - or rather, on the church - over the effigies of a Sir Lionel and Lady Le Mesurier, who had lived and loved and died before the Tudors began to reign in England. As he looked at the still stone faces, he wondered whether Sir Lionel had married for love or for lands, and whether 'Dame Eleanor, his wife' had had long or short eyelashes. It did not matter now to Sir Lionel, Jack mused, as he looked at the old warrior in his age-long slumber, whether his marriage had brought fresh money to the coffers or fresh fields to the estate of Greystone; but even now it must matter to him - somewhere and somehow - if he sold his birthright of love for a mess of pottage, or if he made himself a better man for time and for eternity by choosing the best and letting the second-best go by.

As Jack sat in the quaint old pew, among the monuments of dead and gone Le Mesuriers, he threw off the paralysing effect of his uncle's cultured sarcasm; and he felt that those sleeping ancestors of his must have had a nobler creed and a wider charity than he who now reigned at Greystone in their stead, or they would never have fought like heroes and lived like Englishmen, and have gone to their rest with that calm smile upon their carved faces. And he made up his mind that those brave simple soldiers were worth a hundred of the sneering little cynic who now filled their place and bore their name, and that it was far better to follow in their footsteps than in his."

(A Double Thread - 1899)

Journeys' End

"A mile or two to the west of the border line, where cheerful and comfortable Mershire gives place to proud and picturesque Salopshire, there stood in the latter half of the last century - and for the matter of that had been standing for nearly half-a-dozen centuries previously - the Church and Castle of Journeys' End. For a considerable portion of that period there had been standing the ancient Priory as well; but when this story opens, all that remained of the beautiful and venerable building was a pile of ruins scattered about, in that well-ordered confusion of which Time alone knows the secret, between the Church and the sheet of water known as the upper pool.

The history of the place was a romantic one. Early in that dim period of history roughly described as the Middle Ages, (though exactly what they were in the middle of I have never been able to ascertain) two brothers, Fulke and Roger de Purefoy - having fought for their faith in the Crusades - came back to England to spend the remainder of their days in that peace which they both desired and deserved; and they selected for this purpose a piece of land in the midst of the richly-wooded district lying to the south-west of the old Roman road - old even in those days - leading from Dover to the north-western shore. The King granted them the portion of land that they desired, and they named it Journeys' End, since it was here that their long and weary journeyings found an end at last. Each of the brothers shaped this end according to his own particular needs. Fulke, the elder, builded himself a goodly Castle, where he married and had children and found rest for his soul in the domestic happiness of ordinary human nature; whilst Roger, the younger, raised a fair Church and Priory, where he rejoiced and refreshed his way-worn spirit in the rarer and purer atmosphere of the religious life.

Journeys' End had many natural advantages, being situated upon a sort of triangular peninsula formed by a narrow river which flowed round two sides of it; and it lay on the outskirts of that great forest which, four centuries later, sheltered a fugitive king from his foes. Therefore it commanded a good supply of wood and water as well as of pasturage. Also it was not too far away from the haunts of what in those days was accounted as civilization. It lay only ten miles on the one side from the ancient market-town of Silverhampton, where a Mercian princess had built to the glory of God a convent and a collegiate church; and on its other side it took a good horseman barely two hours by Shrewsbury clock to ride into Shrewsbury town.

The Purefoy brothers did not, however, allow this little river to remain a little river long. By means of huge dams a two corners of the triangle they surrounded their peninsula with a wide, semi-circular lake; and at the western point - where a steep waterfall had originally been - they placed a great weir, thus separating the lake into two divisions, known as the upper and the lower pools. At the beginning of the upper pool and at the north east corner of the triangle, stood the Church and Priory, so that these were close to the King's highway, which highway formed the third side of the peninsula. At the western point - the point farthest from the road - stood the Castle: a fine, mediaeval building surrounding the three sides of a square courtyard. This courtyard faced east, and commanded a pretty if not extensive view of the upper pool, the park, and the Church and Priory; but the rooms on the other side of the Castle looked into a flower-garden 'whose dwelling was the light of setting suns'; and beyond this garden were the weir and waterfall which connected the upper and the lower pools. Owing to its position at the apex of the triangle the Castle was practically moated on three sides; whilst its fourth was guarded by a gateway defending the courtyard.

While the upper pool was a calm and smiling lake with meadows sloping to its edge on either side - a place indeed of green pastures and still waters - the lower pool lay in a deep and shady gorge, the banks of which were covered with trees and wild flowers. Snowdrops, daffodils, periwinkles, and bluebells in turn laid their foundation of chrysolite, jasper, amethyst and sapphire: all to be supplanted in the autumn by a golden pavement of fallen leaves. At least this is what happened every year of the last century, so it may be presumed that it likewise happened in the bygone days when Fulke and Roger de Purefoy reigned at Journeys' End. And to me - to whom Nature had always been a picture-book illustrating the letterpress of eternal Truth - it seemed that the green pastures and still waters of the upper pool set forth as in an allegory the perfect peace of the life which Roger de Purefoy had chosen when he built the Priory on its banks; whilst the lights and shades, the depths and shallows, the changing colours of the lower pool, were a type of the more varied existence which fell to the lot of the older brother when he selected the life of the hearth in preference to that of the cloister.

Though Nature remained pretty much the same through the march of the centuries, Man did not. The Priory held its own until the Eighth Henry took its own from it by force, appropriating the same to his unlawful and unauthorized uses; then it gradually fell into ruins, the beautiful chapel alone remaining as the parish church of the village of Journeys' End. The secular part of the estate changed owners many times, until it was finally purchased by Robert Fleming, the first Lord Merchester, towards the close of the eighteenth century. By that time the Castle had altered a great deal since Fulke de Purefoy's days. True, the two wings at the north and south extremities remained much as they had always been, with their small, thick-walled rooms and their spiral staircases; but the western front had been pulled down and rebuilt according to the fair tradition of the Jacobean age; and at a still later date the courtyard had been covered over and transformed into the large halls and spacious saloons of early Georgian times. The great gateway had disappeared altogether; but between the park and the high road which formed the base of the triangle and divided the one end of the semi-circular lake from the other, there ran a low wall, built of the red-brown stone of the Midlands. So that - what with wall and water - the triangle was still separated from the outer world as a little kingdom in itself; though by this time its colonial possessions stretched out for a considerable distance on all sides.

There were two carriage-drives up to the Castle from the main road, each a mile in length, the one lying alongside the upper pool, and the other alongside the lower one. The former ran by the Church and the ruins of the Priory, with the greensward of the park on the one hand and the calm surface of the lake upon the other: a veritable way of peace, and beautiful at all times, especially when the sun was setting behind the Castle, transfiguring its mediaeval turrets and Jacobean minorets into the similitude of some fair city set beyond the limit of earthly care and sorrow, and transforming the placid pool into a sea of glass mingled with fire. The other drive was totally different in character, leading through the green twilight of the beech-woods which overhung the red sandstone cliff and looking down into the mysterious darkness of the deep pool at its foot; yet exquisitely beautiful in its own way, when the green twilight was dappled with the spring sunshine, and the ground was covered with flowers; and again in the autumn days, when the beech-trees laid their red and gold carpet, and the sky showed blue between their bare branches."

(The Lower Pool - 1923)

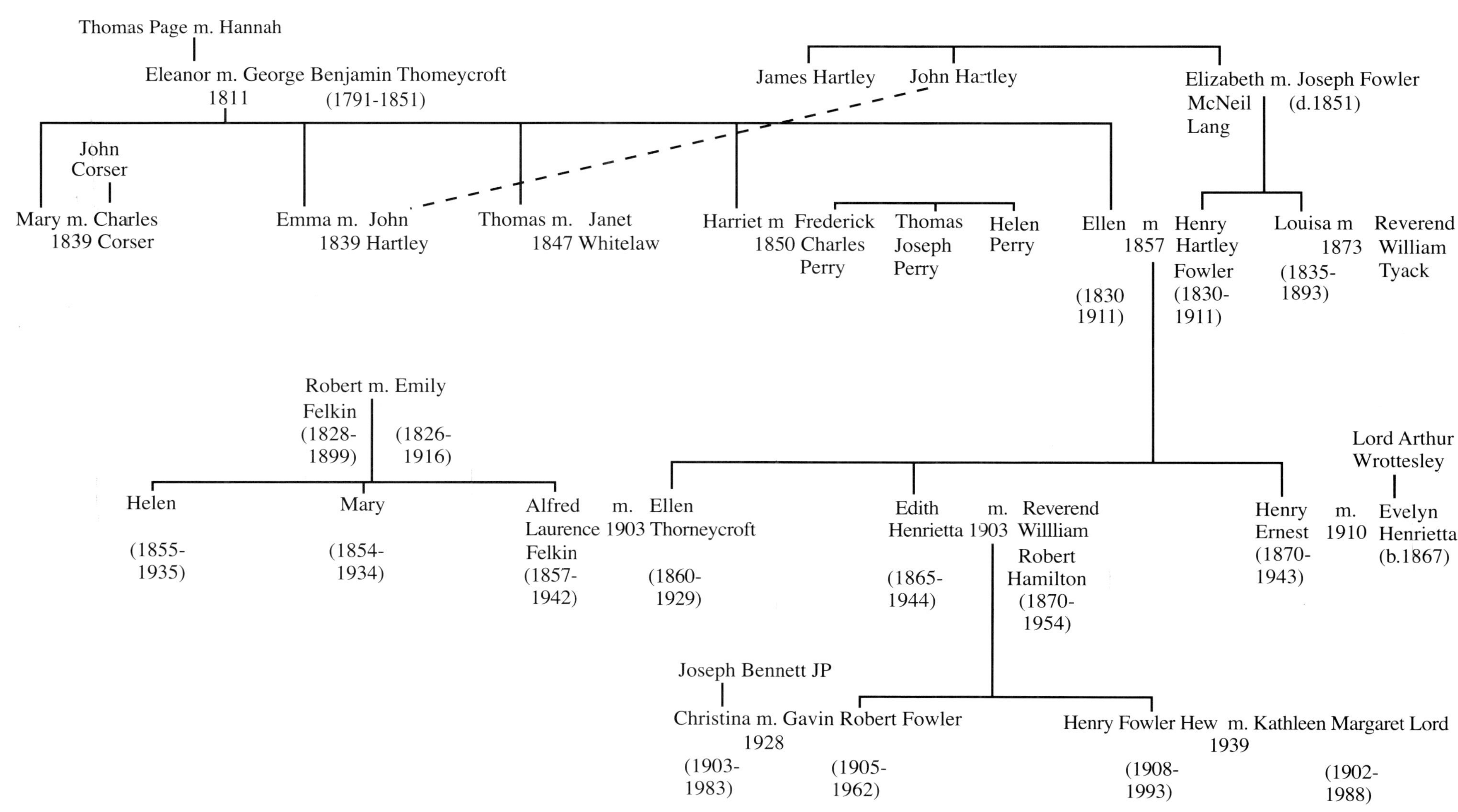
The Fowler and Thorneycroft Families
Thomas Page m. Hannah
Eleanor m. George Benjamin Thomeycroft
1811 (1791-1851)
James Hartley
John Hartley
Elizabeth m. Joseph Fowler
McNeil Lang (d.1851)
John Corser
Mary m. Charles
1839 Corser
Emma m. John
1839 Hartley
Thomas m. Janet
1847 Whitelaw
Harriet m Frederick
1850 Charles Perry
Thomas Joseph Perry
Helen Perry
Ellen m
1857 Henry Hartley Fowler
(1830 1911)
(1830- 1911)
Louisa m
1873 Reverend William Tyack
(1835- 1893)
Robert m. Emily
Felkin
(1828- 1899)
(1826- 1916)
Helen
(1855- 1935)
Mary
(1854- 1934)
Alfred Laurence Felkin m. 1903 Ellen Thorneycroft
(1857- 1942)
(1860- 1929)
Edith Henrietta m. 1903 Willliam Reverend Robert Hamilton
(1865- 1944)
(1870- 1954)
Lord Arthur Wrottesley
Henry Ernest m. 1910 Evelyn Henrietta
(1870- 1943)
(b.1867)
Joseph Bennett JP
Christina m. Gavin Robert Fowler
1928
(1903- 1983)
(1905- 1962)
Henry Fowler Hew m. Kathleen Margaret Lord
1939
(1908- 1993)
(1902- 1988)

The Books of Ellen and Edith Fowler

a) Works of Ellen Thorneycroft Fowler

1891 Verses Grave and Gay
1895 Verses Wise or Otherwise
1897 Cupid's Garden
1898 Concerning Isabel Carnaby
1899 A Double Thread
1899 The Man with Transparent Legs - Twenty Six Ideal Stories for Girls
1900 The Farringdons
1900 Love's Argument & Other Poems
1900 The Isabel Carnaby Birthday Book
1901 The Angel and the Demon & others
1901 How to Make an Angel (temperance tract)
1901 Sirius & other stories
1902 Fuel of Fire
1903 Place and Power
1904 Kate of Kate Hall (with A. L. Felkin)
1905 Verse Wise or Otherwise, incorporating Verses Grave and Gay
1906 In Subjection
1908 Miss Fallowfield's Fortune
1910 The Wisdom of Folly
1913 Her Ladyship's Conscience
1915 Ten Degrees Backward
1920 Beauty and Bands
1923 The Lower Pool
1926 Signs and Wonders

b) Works of Edith Henrietta Fowler

1895 The Young Pretenders
1897 The Professor's Children
1897 Hugh's Burden Bundle (religious tract)
1899 A Corner of the West
1901 The World and Winstow
1905 For Richer for Poorer
1912 Life of Henry Hartley Fowler
1915 Patricia
1921 Christabel